Treas

by

KATHLEEN O'FARRELL

Illustrated by Gillian Rose Peace

By the same Author:

For Children: **The Annabelle series**
Polly of Primrose Hill
The Tylers of Tip Street

Published by Gill's Verse Publications
11, Lupin Works, Worcester Road, Kidderminster, Worcs, England.

First Published in Great Britain, 1992.

British Library Cataloguing-in-Publication Data.
Cover photograph by Evelyn M. Corby

DEDICATION

To the beloved memory
of
Richard Michael Tuck

ACKNOWLEDGEMENTS

With acknowledgements to the editors of "The Lady", "People's Friend", and "The Fireside Book", who first published these poems, and my thanks to those readers who have written to me, and who have become friends.

ISBN 0 9511898 7 5
Printed in England by Sales Print Design Ltd.
Kidderminster, Worcestershire, England. Telephone 0562 752561

CONTENTS

THE FIRST DAY

As bright eyed as a robin,
And darting, like a bee,
Wee Timmy donned his coat and gloves,
All eagerness was he.

Although the rain and wind were fierce,
He didn't give two hoots,
Charging valiantly along
In brand-new scarlet boots.

With "Hurry, Mum!" and "Come on, Mum!"
We hastened on our way,
For countless weeks young Tim had dreamed
Of this Red Letter Day.

And as we neared the schoolyard gate,
His hand in mine held fast,
We knew this very special dream
Was realised at last.

But as we entered through the door
His little legs slowed down,
And on that smooth white brow appeared
An apprehensive frown.

"What a lovely place", I said,
"I'm sure school will be fun!"
But oh, he was a little scrap,
When all was said and done!

So small he was, so vulnerable,
That, when we said goodbye,
I turned my face, to hide the tear
That trembled in my eye....

ANGEL OF THE SPRING

Head down, against the wind we go,
Into the dazzle of the snow,
With frozen fingers, frozen feet,
When suddenly, so small and sweet,
We see, in silver-frosted bed,
A little snowdrop hang her head,
Gently fluttering to and fro
Unruffled by the wind and snow.

Her little petals, shining white,
And veined with tender green, delight
Our winter-weary eyes. We know
That snowflakes don't take root and grow,
And yet, no flake of snow could be
More pure, more beautiful than she!
Hark, and in the stillness hear
Her tiny voice, so crystal clear .....

Reminding us, this cheerless day,
That happier times are on their way,
That soon, though winter winds blow cold,
The silver will give way to gold,
And tulip, wallflower, daffodil,
Each little garden plot will fill!
Oh, little flower, what joy you bring,
What promise - angel of the spring!

THE FLOWER SHOW

Our village hall today must surely be
A gardener's dream of heaven, for the flowers,
Set on long trestles, are such joy to see,
Poppies, petunias, blue delphinium towers,
Fragrant carnations, lilies silver-white,
And roses, satin-smooth, of every hue,
To make one gasp, with wonder and delight,
Their beauty old as time, but ever new.
While fuchsias, purple, crimson, pink and cream,
Splendid as cardinals, in their rich array,
Dazzle the eye, though little pansies seem
To touch the heart, in their own special way.
And oh, the perfume, loveliest of all,
Where massed sweet-peas illuminate the hall!

The flower show's over now ... all's packed away,
But still the glory, the remembered pride,
The colour, scent and pageantry, will stay
Within our minds, for many a day to bide.

DREAM HOUSE

Little house, pretty house,
Down a quiet lane,
Whenever I go strolling by
I long for you in vain.

Little house, half-timbered house,
Your garden is a dream,
Behind the stocks and rosy phlox,
The silver lilies gleam.

Little house, sun-dappled house,
Why do I never see
A curl of smoke, a sign of folk,
Or domesticity?

Little house, old-fashioned house,
You've such a peaceful air,
Beneath your thatch the swallows hatch
In sweet contentment there.

Little house, enchanting house,
You beckon like a star,
I wonder who looks after you,
And where your owners are?

Little house, beloved house,
Some sigh for marble halls,
But I would give the world to live
Within your white-washed walls!

THOSE MARIGOLDS

"I'm sick and tired of marigolds!" the lord and master said.
"They take the garden over...my goodness, how they spread!"
Ruthlessly he set to work, to clear the flower-bed.

Oh, little, laughing marigolds, I tried to intercede,
I tried my very hardest, but he simply wouldn't heed.
He treated you exactly like a nasty, noxious weed!

But when the summer flowers had gone, and autumn ruled the land,
A host of little plants appeared, self-seeded, never planned.
The marigolds were back and now, they had the upper hand.

"Oh, what a lovely, cheerful sight!" cried people passing by,
And he, the lord and master, could not possibly decry
The beauty and the brilliance that met his startled eye.

Like children, irrepressible, but really rather fun,
The marigolds were everywhere ...Each small, audacious one
Stood proudly, holding up aloft its golden-orange sun!

And so they stayed, until one day the lord and master said
"I'm clearing out the marigolds - I fancy something red".
So now our garden's all ablaze - with salvias instead.

But still I dream of marigolds, and just the other day
I saw a cottage garden, where the marigolds held sway,
And oh, the glory and the gold! They took my breath away.

BIRD AND BLOSSOM

A blackbird, on a cherry bough,
Pipes up, and sings "It's Springtime now",
Where pearly blossoms, every one,
Are luminous in April's sun.

With yellow beak, and burnished wings,
Half-lost in cherry-bloom he sings;
What prettier sight could ever be
Than blackbird in a cherry tree?

But when the wind blows, loud and strong,
And nearly drowns the blackbird's song,
The satiny petals, all around,
Sigh, and flutter to the ground.

Then on the grass, like drifts of snow,
We see the dazzling cherry-blow;
So delicate it is, so fair
One hesitates to venture there.

But still the blackbird whistles on,
Until the light of day has gone,
Outlined against the azure sky,
He gratifies both ear and eye.

Through sun and wind and rain he'll sing
His lovely tribute to the spring,
Until it seems that bird and tree
Are merged in one sweet entity.

THE EYES OF INNOCENCE

When you are only four years old,
And all the world seems sparkling new,
Every little star above
Shines just for you.

And when you're coming up to five,
And fairy tales are your delight,
Each one, though ages old, rings true,
Its image bright.

At six years old, so clever then,
You like to help, and find such joy
In putting cherries on a cake,
And many a little, homely ploy.

But when you come to seven, it seems
Your dreams take on a sterner touch,
Monsters, and magic spells, that merge
With dragons, dinosaurs, and such.

And oh, it's such a lovely world,
When you reach the age of ten...
If only I could see it now
As I did then!

IN A COUNTRY CHURCH

Oh, what a quiet pleasure it can be
To spend an hour in sweet tranquillity
In some old country church, where time stands still,
Where nothing changes - nothing ever will.

The great iron latch, on ancient oaken door
Opens to shadowed porch, with stone-flagged floor;
Then, hushed and humble, on a gentle tide
Of peace and stillness, we are drawn inside.
A cherished place... We know, instinctively,
That many hands have laboured, for we see
Well-polished pews, and brasses gleaming bright,
The altar-linen crisp and snowy-white,
While cottage garden flowers and cool green fern
Are beautifully arranged in vase and urn.
The stained-glass windows have old tales to tell
Of childhood saints we know and love full well;
From jewel-rich panes soft colours filter through,
Violet and crimson, emerald, gold and blue,
To fall like benedictions in the gloom,
And scatter rainbows on a cold grey tomb
Where, ever-glorious, stretched out side by side,
Lie knight-crusader and his lady bride.

Churchwarden comes (black cassock, silver hair)
To tell us old Miss Moffat has a flair
For doing flowers - she's done them many a year,
And no-one else would dare to interfere!
"She comes religiously, rain, snow, or sun,"
He says, unconscious of his little pun,
Then bustles off, some errand to fulfill,
Leaving us free to wander at our will.
Upon the walls, the tablets plainly show
What splendid people lived here long ago.
We read them solemnly, and wonder why
Folk were so virtuous in days gone by!

Small, friendly church, among whose sheltering trees
The wild doves call; for countless centuries
Your staunch grey walls, your sturdy tower have stood
Serving both deity and common good!
We say farewell...the summer sun sinks low,
And round your belfry, in the afterglow,
The swallows circle, everything looks fair,
So lovely, so serene, in golden air...

WILD POPPIES

Though the poets sing your praises,
Farmers look on you with scorn,
When you thread your scarlet ribbons
Through their fields of ripening corn.
Little poppies, silken poppies,
Pert and pretty as you please,
Like tiny Romanies you greet us,
Red skirts fluttering, in the breeze.

Black-eyed poppies, ever cheerful,
Bright as paint, and full of fun,
How it lifts the heart to see you,
Dancing gaily in the sun!
Though you cannot vie in beauty
With your sisters, it is true,
No other flower can hold a candle
To the brilliance of your hue.

Evocative of deeds of glory,
In a darker, bygone year,
Though bitter-sweet the thoughts you kindle,
One and all we hold you dear.
And many a tired old face will soften,
Remembering some well-loved name,
At the sight of one wild poppy,
Glowing, steadfast as a flame.

HOMEWORK

"We've got to write a poem," she said,
"For English homework, Mum".
And then, for half an hour she sat
And frowned, and bit her thumb.
"I simply don't know what to write"
She sighed. "It's hard for me,
Instead of thinking lovely thoughts,
I'd sooner climb a tree.
The singing, dancing summertime
Is full of little wings;
I want to run and shout outdoors,
With all the happy things.
Perhaps I'll write one by and by,
But now, I'm off to play,"
She said, and pen and dog-eared book
Were swiftly stowed away.
"I'll never be a girl for poems,"
She cried, with real regret,
And under cloudy, golden hair
Grey eyes looked sad - and yet,
As off she skipped, on slender legs,
She was, in very truth,
Herself a singing, dancing poem,
A poem entitled "Youth".

I SEE YOU STILL

Somctimes, coming through the door,
I think I see you there,
Relaxing, so contentedly,
In your favourite chair.

Your baccy-jar is on the shelf,
And there it's going to stay,
I couldn't bear to part with it,
No matter what folk say.

Your cherished pipe, your spectacles,
Your books, your slippers, too,
In keeping them, I seem to keep
A little bit of you.

These day-to-day, familiar things
I now hold very dear,
For, in their simple homeliness,
They seem to bring you near.

That's why I smile, much comforted,
When coming through the door,
Because, deep in my heart, I know
You've just gone on before!

LINGERING BEAUTY

When breezes stir the tender blades of corn,
Like gentle fingers, idly running through
A dryad's pale green tresses, and the sky
Is one great, cloudless vault of harebell-blue;
When scarlet poppies quiver on the brink
Of motorways, and drifts of daisies glow
Snow-white, on railroad banks, and song-birds flute
From dawn till dusk, how good it is to know
Such beauty cannot fade, but lingers on
Deep in the heart, though summertime be gone.

THE CHRISTENING ROBE

A century or more ago,
By lamp, or candlelight,
Loving fingers fashioned you,
From cotton, crisp and white,
With stitches, oh so very small,
It's hard to see them there at all!

As peerless as a drift of snow,
Or cherry-bloom in May,
Countless babes have you adorned
Upon their special day;
Each generation handing down
With pride, its cherished christening gown.

Embroidered with the tiniest flowers,
And trimmed with narrow lace,
You but enhance the beauty of
Each gentle baby face;
With handiwork so fine to see,
Yet of such sweet simplicity.

The passing years were kind, it seems,
For perfect you've remained,
Since that first christening, ages gone,
When Queen Victoria reigned,
And, in the years to come, I vow
You will be treasured - just as now!

MOUNTAIN PEACE

I love a summer evening, when the dark
Comes, oh so softly, down the mountainside,
Enfolding all the fields, the little farms,
In gentle, purple arms.

When all across the valley, lamps are lit,
Ribbons of light, so friendly and so warm,
While every bush and tree
Is cloaked in mystery.

When high above, among ten thousand stars,
The moon floats, shining, through wind-ruffled clouds,
And stresses of the day
Just slip away.

Oh, blissful summer evening, when the hush
Of age-old mountains like a blessing falls,
And all life seems
Fashioned from lovely dreams....

TREASURES

Granny has a treasure, it's something very old,
A little locket, worn and thin,
With both her parents' photos in,
And made of purest gold.

Grandad has a treasure, it's his greenhouse, where he grows
Flowers and vegetables, to share
With friends and neighbours ....I declare
It keeps him on his toes!

Father has a treasure, it's a silver cup he won
For running..... Oh, we nearly burst
With cheering, when he came in first
In our town's Marathon!

Susan has a treasure, it's her pleasure and her pride;
She's saved for years, and now she's bought
The newest, shiniest, smartest sort
Of bicycle to ride!

And yet the dearest treasure, that means everything to Mother,
Is just a tiny satin shoe,
Scarcely worn, so soft and blue,
It's sad to think we never knew
Our darling baby brother.........

THE DOLL MUSEUM

Why do I feel a pang to see you there,
Seated so primly in a patient row,
With cheeks of porcelain, long, flowing hair,
Angelic smile, and mouth like Cupid's bow?
Demurely dressed, in taffeta and lace,
With cool, pale faces delicate as flowers,
What do you think of us who haunt this place?
How do you like this brave new world of ours?

The skies are pierced with flashing silver wings,
Beyond the door the juggernauts roll by,
But you must dream of older, lovelier things,
The nursery fire with bright flames leaping high,
White-aproned Nanny, capable and kind,
Small girls with shining ringlets tightly curled,
Now gone for ever, leaving you behind,
Gentle and faded in an alien world.

Why do I feel a pang? Within this room
I seem to sense your longing and your pain,
For memory lingers, sweet as old perfume,
Of happier days that will not come again.
Once you were cherished, given pretty names,
By those small girls, who loved you long ago,
You shared their secrets, joined in all their games,
And brought them consolation in their woe.

All vanished now..... Forgotten by us all,
But not by you, who never will forget.
In buttoned boots, and holland overall,
I'm very sure that you can see them yet.
Perhaps, by night, those little ones return,
When all is hushed, and shuttered tight the door,
Running with outstretched arms, because they yearn
To hug you, kiss you, love you as before.........

TRANQUILLITY

Tranquillity... it's such a lovely word,
Such gentle imagery its mention brings,
A drift of daisies, fluttering in the breeze,
A butterfly, with outspread velvet wings,
Sunning itself in some quiet corner, where
Only a falling petal stirs the air.

Tranquillity....It's something to be found
Under the willow fronds, where swans glide by
Upon a placid lake, that mirrors both
The graceful birds, and limpid summer sky;
Or in dim, ferny woods, where, crystal-clear,
The bluebells chime.... though only children hear!

Tranquillity..... it conjures up a scene
Of bright stars shining on untrodden snow,
Of little, ancient churches, where the air,
Fragrant with lilies, breathes of long ago;
Or some green field, where little rabbits play,
In the deep hush that comes at close of day.

Yet, in mean city streets, we still may find
Tranquillity.... if we have peace of mind.

THE BAKER'S SHOP

Sometimes, I wistfully recall
The baker's shop when I was small,
It stood upon the village square,
And nothing ever could compare
With cottage-loaves and Sally Lunns,
And two-a-penny currant buns,
All freshly made by baker Jack,
In the bakehouse at the back.
Behind the counter, freckled Nell
Knitted through each quiet spell,
And once, when someone asked for bread,
"Hang on a minute, dear," she said,
"I <u>must</u> get my decreasings done,
And this row is a tricky one!"
While in the window proudly sat
The most enormous tabby cat,
With tarts and doughnuts piled up high
On either side .... His golden eye
Shone so benignly, none would dare
To comment on his presence there.
I loved the baker's shop when young,
And often heard its praises sung,
Until, (it was a dreadful shame!)
A ministerial person came.
"What's this?" he cried, in shocked surprise,
"A cat, among the cakes and pies!
As Health Inspector, I decree
That cat must go - immediately!"
So pussy went ... and in a trice
The shop was over-run by mice!

We had to buy our bread from town,
When they closed the baker's down.
It never tasted half so good
As Jack's - and no bread ever would!

PUFFING BILLY

In youth's bright heyday, long ago, my little friends and I
Would sit upon the garden fence, to watch the trains go by,
And when we glimpsed a plume of smoke, we'd cheer with might and main,
As though to welcome all aboard our splendid "bonfire" train.

We'd see it coming from afar, so small, so trim and neat,
Chugging through the countryside, with steady, rhythmic beat,
And how excitedly we waved, as nearer still it came,
So mighty, so magnificent, its cabin lit with flame!

Oh, Puffing Billy, how our ears were deafened as you flew
Between the steep embankments where a million daisies grew,
Big, snowy daisies, golden-eyed ... I seem them shining yet,
They symbolise those childhood days I never will forget.

Sometimes, the shovel in his hand, the stoker would wave back,
But best of all was when our train was halted on the track,
And oh, the heady, acrid smell of coal-dust on the air,
As Billy shuddered to a stop, and sparks flew everywhere!

We had such simple pleasures then, and none of us could boast
Of travelling any further than the Kent or Sussex coast,
But in our dreams we journeyed far, cross land, and sea, and sky;
No wonder that our pulses raced, when Billy thundered by!

HONEY FOR TEA

"HONEY FOR SALE", the notice said,
Pinned to a gnarled old tree,
And I thought it would be rather nice
To have scones and honey for tea.
So I trod the ancient, stone-flagged path
To a friendly cottage door,
Where a black dog leapt to welcome me,
And kittens played, three or four.
The beehives under the orchard bough
Stood in a shining row,
While petals around their slatted walls
Fluttered like pale pink snow.
The air was full of the scents of spring,
And a cheerful, industrious hum,
While a blackbird sang in a lilac bush....
Oh, I felt so glad I'd come!
The countrywoman, cosily plump,
Who greeted me, seemed to match
Her snug little house, with its diamond panes
Twinkling beneath the thatch.
Her smile was warm; with sturdy gait,
The jar of honey she brought,
And the price, though rather high, I paid
Without a second thought.
Then back I took, to my high-rise flat,
In the city, not merely honey,
But a glimpse of a lovely, forgotten world,
Too precious to buy with money!

SNOWFALL

The strong, clear light, unearthly bright
Invades each corner of my room.
Outside I see, so vividly,
The snowflakes fall, like cherry-bloom.

The old folk sigh, with anguished eye,
But children don warm caps and gloves,
And lift the latch, and run to catch
White feathers from a million doves.

See now unfurl, like smoky pearl,
Old winter's backcloth. To and fro,
In dance unending, twisting, bending,
Tiny ballerinas go.

Young lambs at play, white buds of May,
Small craft atoss on fairy sea.....
What but the snow could thus bestow
Such ever-changing imagery?

What can compare? No lily fair,
Nor windflower. Why, the whitest rose
Would hide its face, where fine as lace
A little, shining snowflake glows!

The age of gold is gone, we're told,
A hundred thousand moons ago.
But turn the page ... the silver age
Dawns, crystal-radiant with the snow!

REFLECTIONS

I don't remember where we were, or what the time of day,
Though spring was surely at its height, for all along the way
The lilac and laburnum flamed - and oh, the crimson may!
When suddenly we chanced upon the most delightful scene,
A lake, all fringed with flowering shrubs, and willows, golden-green.

Slowly, a swan went gliding past, its feathers silvery-white,
And in that dappled, dreamy place, of shade and flickering light,
All was doubly beautiful, for bushes, blossom-bright,
Glowed, not only on the banks, but in the lake below,
In glorious shades of dusky rose, and gold, and indigo.

So still it was, so quiet it was .... it shook the heart to see
Mirrored in the water clear each gently quivering tree,
While, with the swan, a shadow-swan was keeping company!
Two little worlds, enchanting worlds, so tranquil and so fair,
One, in the limpid lake below, and one in sunlit air!

I don't remember where we were, yet I recall that day
When everywhere seemed heady with the fragrance of the may,
And many a time I long to go and find that woodland way,
To tread that mossy path again, that dim, green, ferny track,
That led us, in its wild, sweet way, to fairyland, and back.......

THE TRANQUIL YEARS

On such a day as this, when everywhere
Sparkles and shimmers in the crystal air,
How good it is, we tell ourselves, to be
Older in years yet young at heart, and free!
Unrushed, unheeding, through the sun or snow,
When nature beckons, and beguiles, we go,
Hugging the thought that now there's time to do
A myriad things we've always wanted to.

While savouring each brand-new, precious day,
And making plans, it's wonderful, we say,
To realize we need not rush or tear
For bus or train, to get from here to there.
For now, when we have quit the frenzied race,
And may enjoy life's gentler leisured pace,
We see through different eyes, and each day find
New interests, new delights, for heart and mind.

Old, cherished dreams, too lovely to forget,
May still materialize, it seems ... and yet,
We'd trade it all, (oh yes, we wish in vain!),
For one brief spell of being young again.

THOUGHTS IN A STATELY HOME

Booklets in hand, and close behind our guide,
Jesting and jostling, like a human tide
We surge, both young and old, a motley crew
Eager to purchase tickets, and pass through
This time-worn portal, where for two brief hours
We may explore a different world from ours.

Inside, all round us, cabinets reveal
Beauty to make our inner senses reel;
In awesome hush, we stand, and gaze up to
A miracle of gold and pink and blue,
A painted vista of a star-strewn sky,
Where, crowned with blossoms, rosy cherubs fly.

Do you resent us, you who used to dwell
Within this noble house, who knew so well
This lofty hall, these rooms, this graceful stair?
Proud, silent ghosts, your portraits hanging there
Seem to gaze down, with cool, appraising eye
On us, the trespassers, who saunter by.

Do not disdain us ... For so short a while
We share the splendour of your stately pile,
Charmed by the sparkling crystal, silver, gold,
Treasures from East and West, their worth untold;
And sometimes wondering, do we dream or see
Fragmentary pictures of what used to be?
Periwig, powder, patch, and ringlet-curl,
Dazzle of diamonds, softly glimmering pearl,
Flunkies in crimson, goblets raised on high,
Fine lace, and panniered skirts that float on by,
Flickering candles, ivory brocade,
White cap and homespun gown, of serving-maid....

And those faint sounds we hear .... a fluttering fan,
A lover's sigh, the same since time began,
A snatch of some old song, that echoes still
Down through the centuries, and always will;
Rustle of satin, tap of dancing feet,
And harpsichord, its music clear and sweet,
Touching the heart with haunting old refrain
Of days gone by, that will not come again.

Oh, spirits of the past, we say adieu,
Yet here remains so much to comfort you,
For though life's transient, and you are gone,
The loveliness you knew lives on and on!

ENCOUNTER WITH AN OLD ACQUAINTANCE

My dear old friend, with what delight
Our comradeship has been renewed;
For many a time I've thought of you,
So wistfully, in pensive mood.
In ages gone, my trusted guide,
My mentor, you would take my hand,
To lead me down enchanted roads,
Into many an unknown land.
Then, with the passing years, alas,
Old friends, discarded, dropped away,
Along with all those roseate dreams
That never saw the light of day.
What bliss, then, in that dusty shop,
To find you ... for in very truth,
You were the joy - beloved book -
And inspiration of my youth!

PUPPY LOVE

I met them strolling on the heath,
The tall young man, and Rory,
And straightaway I lost my heart,
Just like an old, sweet story!

Young Rory was a Labrador,
So handsome, four months old,
With dreamy eyes, and wagging tail,
Soft coat of palest gold.

The stranger said his name was Bill,
He seemed quite keen to talk,
And said perhaps next day I'd care
To join them on their walk.

It seemed he lived quite near to me,
So I arranged to meet
And stroll with them, for love had come
And swept me off my feet.

The briar-roses were in bloom,
And daisies glimmered white,
Where Rory frolicked, joyfully,
In unrestrained delight.

Though Bill was witty, wise and kind,
With such a gentle gaze,
I paid him little heed, because
Of Rory's winsome ways.

When I called Rory "darling dog",
And hugged him close today,
"I wish I were a Labrador!"
Sighed Bill, and turned away.

It set me thinking .... could it be -
The coming days will tell -
That, in my heart, there's room enough
For dear old Bill, as well?

OUR RACHEL

What a honeypot is Rachel,
Now she's reached the age of two,
With hair as pale as primroses,
And eyes of laughing blue!
She's a terror, she's a torment,
Always in a joyous whirl;
Who'd believe that so much chaos
Could be caused by one small girl?

What a scallywag is Rachel!
Strong men cannot hide their fear,
When the sound of fairy footsteps
Tells them tiny Rachel's near.
She's a trial, a tribulation,
Yet you'd need a heart of stone
To resist that little poppet
Sending kisses down the phone.

What a tireless tot is Rachel!
On the go till set of sun,
She's not one small girl, but several,
Good and bad, rolled into one.
Now, a tomboy bent on mischief,
Now demure in frilly dress,
What matter, be she imp or angel,
I could never love her less!

THE ROCKING HORSE

Oh, how I longed when I was small,
Though the longing was all in vain,
For a rocking horse, old fashioned, of course,
With a wonderful flowing mane.
He'd be Dobbin, or Ned, with a saddle of red,
And a bushy tail, silvery white,
And oh, how his dappled coat would shine,
As he nuzzled his dear old face to mine,
When we galloped into the night!
Off we'd go, in the firelight's gleam,
To a fairy wood by a fairy stream,
In that far-off, fabulous, childhood dream
That I cherished with such delight.

It never came true. Old Dobbin or Ned
Never materialized .... instead,
I'd receive a doll, or a book, or game
Whenever a birthday, or Christmas came,
(For times were hard, they said.)
Yet now, belatedly though it seems,
I've purchased the rocking horse of my dreams,
(Sheer folly, my friends will say!)
A beautiful horse, old fashioned, of course,
For when grandchildren come to stay.
And when they hug him, and stroke his mane,
Adrian, Susie, and Tabitha Jane,
And the little ones who come after,
I'll feel as young and as blithe as they;
And even when they are far away,
In my heart will echo for many a day
Their innocent, joyous laughter.

A YORKSHIRE GLEN

So well I remember ..... I told myself then,
No scenic splendour, forest or fen,
Could ever surpass that little glen;
A secret place, in a moorland fold,
Hidden from view, like a crock of gold.

Deep-drowned in honey, on either side
The small hills drowsed ... Their summer pride
Of heather flowed like a silken tide.
And oh, the sheen in the noonday sun
Of blossom, purple and rose in one!

From ferny bed, on the moorland's crown,
The crystal brook came tumbling down,
Over the boulders clean and brown;
While black-faced sheep, with scarce a sound,
Clustered, cropping the mossy ground.

Toadstools, as vivid as orange-peel,
Grew thick beneath my careless heel;
Would their small goblin roofs reveal
A little magic world, were I
Insensitive enough to pry?

And now, in the bustling throng, I yearn
To follow my impulse and return
To that leafy haven of flower and fern!
But oh, would I ever find you again,
Little beautiful, far-away, fairy-tale glen?

THE DONKEY-TRAP

My luggage packed, departure nigh,
There at my garden gate stood I,
To watch a donkey-trap go by.
Soon I must leave to catch my plane,
And yet I paused .... Like April rain
Came tiny hoof-beats down the lane.

Within the yellow-painted trap,
In spotted scarf and ancient cap,
Sat Joe, the reins upon his lap;
A gnome-like creature, small and spry,
With weathered cheek and roguish eye.
I smiled. He nodded in reply.

From where he came I cannot tell,
Although by sight I knew him well,
And everyone loved Daisybelle!
All eyes and ears, her soulful gaze
And dozy, dreamy donkey ways
Seemed to belong to other days.

As neither of them seemed to care
For speed, they made a perfect pair.
Old Joe had such a leisured air!
And suddenly I longed to ride
Between the hedgerows, by his side,
Into the singing summertide.

For, in this age of jumbo-jet,
When people fuss and fume and fret,
And clamour: 'Faster! Faster yet!'
It makes one wonder, are not we
Hurrying, scurrying needlessly,
Headlong into eternity?

Then comes an urge to quit the race,
To travel at the gentle pace
Of Daisybelle. Her patient face
Looked back at me, as though to say
'Join us, we have the livelong day
To reach our goal, five miles away'.

But there I stood and watched them go,
The small grey donkey, wise old Joe,
And thought: 'Tomorrow, Tokyo!'
Clip-clop, clip-clop along the lane
They went ... I never will explain
That sense of loss, that stab of pain ....

SONG OF SILENCE

There is a silence in the woods,
A silence comforting and deep,
When birds are mute, and every tree
Stands motionless, in shadowed sleep.
When every little woodland flower
Is under summer's drowsy spell,
And many an ancient, mossy bough
An old, bewitching tale could tell.
Then, in the calm and dreaming air,
Along each dappled, ferny way,
The peace of centuries gone by
Melts into stillness of today;
And in that hush, so absolute,
There sometimes echoes, soft and clear,
A greenwood song, which only those
With ears, and hearts, attuned, may hear ......

THE MIRACLE

It's ten o'clock and we climb the stair,
To peep at our little lad sleeping there,
So small, so still, in his painted bed,
With soft, bright hair on the pillow spread;
And we ask ourselves, in a puzzled way,
Who did those mischievous things today?

Who rubbed strawberry jam in his hair,
And squashed a tomato all over his chair?
Who broke an egg-cup, and, worst of all,
Scribbled with lipstick all over the wall?
Who stole the nuts off the trifle, and who
Hid half a cream-bun in his father's shoe?

Who chased the terrified tot next door
With the biggest spider you ever saw?
Who flooded the kitchen? Who can explain
Why the clock will never cry 'Cuckoo' again?
Not Jonathan, dreaming so sweetly there,
Cheek-to-cheek with his Paddington Bear!

Each night it happens. With snail-like tread,
A naughty, wee scoundrel creeps up to bed.
Yet, when we peep when the moon is high,
The loveliest miracle meets our eye.
The imp has vanished .... All rosy and fair,
A little boy angel slumbers there!

A SUSSEX WINDMILL

High on the hilltop, gazing down
On the turrets and towers of a grey-walled town,
The windmill stands with his arms outspread,
The white gulls wheeling around his head.
On either hand, where the Downs unfold,
Ripples of ripe corn, silver-gold,
Stretch as far as the eye can view
To shimmering waters, hyacinth-blue,
To cliffs, and a boat with a scarlet sail,
While down in the many-steepled vale
The workaday world moves on so fast,
You'd think each moment would be its last,
With hustle and bustle, and grief and care,
But the old mill stands inviolate there,
His labours over ... But does he sigh,
This gentle giant, for days gone by?

Out of the cornfield little mice run,
And rabbits play at the set of sun,
But is there an ache in that faithful heart
To see a horse with a painted cart,
A girl in a long white pinafore,
Stealing a ride, as in days of yore
When, laughing, singing, along each lane
The farmers trundled their sacks of grain,
And Miller was busy, snow-white with flour,
From dawn till dusk in his stalwart tower?
And yet, the windmill is still the pride
And joy of that Sussex countryside.

In brilliant sunshine he seems to blaze
Like a great white knight of olden days,
Or a guardian angel, staunch and bright,
Keeping his vigil day and night,
From early morn when the wavelets curl
Over a sea like mother-of-pearl
Till moonlight dapples the quiet Down
And lights come on in the little town,
Winking and twinkling, row on row,
He has stars above him, and stars below!

Through velvet darkness, through heat and chill,
Firm as a rock stands the ancient mill,
So strong, unchanging, one feels that he
Will be there for all eternity,
High on his hilltop, gazing down,
As though he were blessing the little town.

CLOUDS

Why do people speak of clouds as if they're tiresome things?
When some are soft and beautiful, like angels' feathered wings,
And some, like little sailing boats, float on a sea so blue,
You'd think your cherished ship-of-dreams was coming home to you.

And though they may be menacing, at times so dark and grey,
Their flower-bright colours, shot with gold, enhance the close of day,
Rose-red and lilac, blossom-pink, like drifts of fairy snow,
That fade to palest apple-green, in sunset's afterglow.

And when you're in a place apart, far from the bustling town,
Look up, and watch cloud shadows pass across the quiet Down.
Or over fields of rippling wheat, when harvest time is nigh,
How slowly, how majestically, they move across the sky.

In days of old the children gazed at pictures in the fire,
But now, just look at cloudscapes, and you'll see your heart's desire;
A mountain range, its summit bathed in radiant silver light,
The pinions of a splendid bird, poised in its upward flight.

A white-walled palace, roofed with stars, a city old as time,
Or moon-washed cliffs, or fluffy lambs straight from a nursery rhyme,
For clouds are ever-changing, they're a wonder, a delight,
Our heavens would be dull indeed, with never a cloud in sight!

BIRTHDAY PRESENTS

"What would you like for your birthday, dear?" they asked - he was nearly seven,
With ginger curls, and a cheeky grin, and eyes as blue as Heaven.

He thought for a while, then excitedly: "What I'd really like", he said,
"Is a dinosaur of my very own, to sleep at the foot of my bed.
"And perhaps a magical silver flute, to play me a magical tune,
And a space-suit and helmet, so I could fly in a rocket up to the moon.

And, just for fun, I would love to have a tiny, brown mischievous elf,
Who'd be my friend, and play naughty tricks on everyone, but myself.
Then I'd like my very own aeroplane, a real one, silver and red,
That I could pilot - but small enough to fit in the garden shed.

And a dear little monkey, or better still, a jolly great chimpanzee.
We could play together, and he would sit beside me, for dinner and tea.
And a model yacht, and a motor-boat (with remote controls, of course),
And a donkey, a pony, and - if there's room - a lovely featherfoot horse.

Then chocolate-toffees ... I'd like to have a simply enormous tin,
So that all the boys in the street could come, and dip their fingers in.
But I nearly forgot! If I come down, and find, propped up in the hall,
A beautiful, brand-new bicycle, that would be best of all".

And the grown-ups listened, indulgently, they smiled, and patted his head;
Then they bought him a book, and a pencil-case, and a jigsaw-puzzle instead!

THE PILGRIMS' WAY

Oh, the little lane led me such a dance
Over the hill and down,
But I still kept on, so glad to be
Out in the sunshine, fancy-free,
Away from the clamour of town.

Unchanged, for a thousand years or more,
Past hedges creamy with may,
Through bramble-thickets, and banks of fern,
And dim green woods, it would twist and turn,
As it followed its hallowed way.

For long ago, in the mists of time,
When faith burned bright as a flame,
This old path led to a holy shrine,
And here, imbued with a love divine,
The gentle pilgrims came.

The lane is almost forgotten now,
(Though guide-books list it still),
But sometimes, soft on the blossomy air,
There echoes a fragment of ancient prayer,
As if the sanctity lingers there
Like a blessing, and always will ...

TABBY-TOM

Tabby-Tom is not unique,
You'll find a score like him,
Any day of any week,
Around the city's rim.
He has no class, no pedigree,
And in a judge's eyes,
A cat as commonplace as he
Should never win a prize.
And yet, his deep and rumbling purr,
His dreamy, golden gaze,
His lovely, shining, brindled fur
Inspired this song of praise.

Abandoned several years ago,
A scared and starving stray,
Tabby-Tom limped to and fro,
Until he chanced our way.
We took him in ... I can't forget
The sadness and the strain,
Until the broken hip was set,
And Tom came home again.

The little, scrawny kitten grew
So quickly, after that,
And very soon he turned into
A most delightful cat.
Like pussy-willlow are his paws,
His coat gleams silver-grey,
We never see a sign of claws,
For ever sheathed are they.
Who cares about his ancestry?
Our Tommy's set apart;
I'm sure no cat could ever be
Closer to my heart.

THE POTTING SHED

Dimly, dustily, evoking
Seed and sapling, bud and bloom,
Memories of bygone summers
Haunt this apple-scented gloom.

From a springtime long forgotten,
From an autumn all aglow,
Still an old enchantment lingers,
Round the shovel, fork, and hoe.

Flower-pots, in red towers ascending,
Sacks, and raspberry-canes galore,
Mud-caked boots, and fertiliser,
Watering-can, and wisps of straw ...

Here, in cobwebby contentment,
Tiny, creeping things hold sway,
Where crumpled leaf and faded petal
On the slatted shelf decay.

Homely muddle notwithstanding,
With our inner eyes we see
All the green and golden promise
Of the loveliness to be.

For, no matter what the season,
This is such a friendly place,
All the glory of the garden
Has its birth in this small space.

THE VILLAGE STORE

Sometimes, in reflective mood,
When the past comes back to me,
I recall our village shop
In the days that used to be.

In that dim and fragrant cave,
You could buy just everything,
From cottage loaves to candlesticks,
From babies' bibs to balls of string.

When very young, I loved to go
On messages for this and that,
Some dolly-pegs, a card of pins,
Three bacon-rashers - not too fat!

And what a welcome one received
From Bess, in floral pinafore,
When the little, tinkling bell
Announced one's entry through the door!

No pre-packed food, no serve-yourself,
But Bess would always give advice
On such a multitude of things,
While weighing sago up, or rice.

And wise old Will knew all there was
To know about broad-beans, and such,
For, as a gardener, William had
An undisputed magic touch.

And oh, the lovely, mingled scent
Of polish, oranges, and spice,
Of cheese, and apples, yellow soap,
Cough-candy bars, and sugar-mice!

Sometimes, if I close my eyes,
That haunting scent returns to me,
And I am in our village shop,
Buying ha'penny buns for tea ...

SMALL FRY

"Small Fry" - though it's often heard,
Is such a funny name
For little boys and girls, that some
May wonder whence it came.

Tiddlers, it means, and tiny fish,
Yet somehow calls to mind
Children bursting through the door,
A madcap dog behind.

Dinosaurs, and fairy-tales,
And little gap-toothed faces,
With jars of tadpoles, dotted here
And there, in awkward places.

Fingermarks upon the wall,
A never-ending din,
And great big golden buttercups
Held underneath the chin.

Chicken-pox, and pillow-fights,
First glimpses of the sea,
Small arms reached out, as if to say,
"Please take me on your knee!"

Paddling-pools, and picnics planned
For well-loved teddy-bears,
And dreadful scuffles, ending with
A tumble down the stairs ...

Muddy wellies in the hall,
Wet socks in soggy pile,
With hugs and kisses, unrestrained,
To make it all worth while.

Until one day we look around,
And wistfully deplore
The sad fact that our little ones
Aren't Small Fry any more ...

TRUE LOVE

Last week I had a dreadful shock ... Our vicar came to call,
And Mummy filled a great big box, with jumble for his stall;
Then, in among the clothes and books, she popped my ancient Ted,
"You have so many lovely toys, it's time he went," she said.

And true it was, you couldn't call my Ted a handsome bear,
(I'd cuddled all his fur away, and one eye wasn't there!)
But still I loved him very much, a cherished friend was he,
So shabby to the world at large, yet precious still to me.

Wide-eyed with grief, and disbelief, I watched my teddy go,
And then I cried myself to sleep, three nights in a row,
But secretly, you understand, for big girls shouldn't cry,
So no-one guessed how sad I was, as lonely days went by.

Then came the sale ... One hope there was, one chance and that was all,
Pocket money in my hand, I raced to our church hall,
And there I found my poor old Ted, forlorn as he could be,
For no-one wanted him, it seemed, no, not a soul but me!

The vicar's wife, who ran the stall, (she's really rather nice),
Looked at Ted, then smiled and said that ten pence was his price,
And so I bought my teddy back ... Oh, happy, happy day!
I danced along our village street, and hugged him all the way.

And now I've knitted him a coat, bright red, with matching cap,
No wonder people say he looks a most distinguished chap!
And as for Mum, when she comes in, to tuck me up in bed,
She has to kiss us both good night - me, and my darling Ted!

UNSUNG BEAUTY

Dare one ask why
The accolade that one bestows
On daffodil, or damask rose,
Or frail forget-me-not,
Should not, in beauty's name apply
To every lovely plant that grows,
Without the frills and furbelows,
In a more humble plot?

Though so beautiful within,
Kitchen gardens do not share
The honeyed phrases that elsewhere
Extol their kith and kin.
Yet, as the harvest time draws nigh,
The gardener's mind and heart and eye
Are all refreshed and gladdened by
Smooth contours, satin skin.

A lettuce twinkles, diamond-hung,
After showers of April rain,
While rhubarb shines like pink champagne,
But are their praises ever sung?
The scent of broad-bean flowers in May,
Can almost take one's breath away,
And as to colour, what can vie
With purple-sprouting broccoli?

Green-feathered carrots, row on row,
Tomatoes, with their scarlet glow,
Neat cauliflowers, as cool as snow,
Asparagus like lace ...
The kitchen garden has an air
Of rich abundance everywhere,
Oh, how could Eden be more fair
Than this dear, homely place?

RUSSET, SCARLET AND GOLD

When the last petal has fallen
From the red rose and the white,
And the garden chairs and the paddling-pool
Are put away out of sight,
How lovely to welcome autumn,
As she drifts through the misty air,
With a crown of Michaelmas-daisies
Upon her flame-bright hair!

When summer's glory is over,
And nights grow dark and cold,
Then, in her friendly homespun,
Of russet and scarlet and gold,
With a necklace of hawthorn berries,
And her smoky, purple gaze,
Brave and bewitching autumn
Lights up the woodland ways.

So though we may yearn for summer,
Its sunshine, its skies of blue,
And sigh for magical days gone by,
And all the joys we knew,
Let us sing autumn's praises,
As the leaves come fluttering down,
Autumn, with her tawny hair,
Her Michaelmas-daisy crown!

NO CHOICE

Sometimes, rather wistfully,
I think it might be fun
To choose a kitten for myself,
A very special one.
For though I'm very fond of cats,
Each colour, every sort,
I've never had the option of
A long-haired or a short.

For strays have always made their way
Unbidden, to my door,
Ginger, and grey, and tortoiseshell,
And jet-black cats galore.
Bedraggled, in the pouring rain,
Half-frozen, in the snow,
Who could turn away a cat
With nowhere else to go?

Dear Bunty, Blackie, Tabby-Tom,
And all their furry kin,
Some were very beautiful,
Some battle-scarred and thin,
But when their sad eyes gazed at me,
With such a mute despair,
I'd let these lesser brethren in,
Our hearth and home to share.

And each one, in it's turn, became
A cherished family pet,
Smooth, or fluffy, spotted, striped,
All lovable - and yet,
Although for countless years, I've had
A cat upon my knee,
I've never chosen one of them,
They've always chosen me!

COTTAGE GARDEN

I knew a little garden once, that was a sheer delight,
All poppies and petunias, and lilies silver-white.
Unkempt it was, and gone to seed, and yet it had an air
Of such deep peace and kindliness, one felt a welcome there.

Little pansies, golden-bronze, wine-red, and sapphire-blue,
And flame-tipped spires of mignonette, beneath the windows grew,
While butterflies were everywhere - they'd constantly alight
To sun themselves, with outspread wings, upon the petals bright.

One hedge there was of rosemary, another one of box,
With lad's love in the border, and a mass of homely phlox,
And oh, the clamour of the bees upon a summer's day,
Among the silken hollyhocks, the clouds of bride's bouquet!

The kitchen garden, just behind, had not an inch of space,
For rhubarb, raspberries, and beans, all jostled for a place,
While chickens wandered at their will, and from a gnarled old tree
A bird would pipe a merry tune, especially for me.

That garden wasn't planned at all, as gardens are today,
With here a plant, and there a bush, set out in neat array.
But oh, I thought it beautiful, when I was very small,
A place of dreams and memories - it held me in its thrall.

WISHFUL THINKING

Sometimes, when I gaze at Mum,
With baby on her knee,
I dream about the time she was
A little girl like me.

A little girl whose name was Jill,
A tomboy, so they say,
Who'd turn a cartwheel with the best,
And sing the livelong day.

A girl with two long pony-tails,
A cheeky, laughing face,
Whose school reports said: "Good at games,
But spelling's a disgrace".

Everybody likes my mum,
She's sensible and kind,
A wee bit bossy, truth to tell,
But I don't really mind.

For every now and then I glimpse
A twinkle in her eye,
And I can see that little girl
She was in days gone by.

A girl who loved to hop and skip,
To clamber up a tree ...
Oh, how I wish I'd known my mum
When she was small, like me!

THE SHIRE HORSE

Is there anything more splendid than a Shire horse at the show?
For if there is, then I for one would dearly love to know.
All silky, shining ribbons, and rosettes and gleaming brass,
With great, big feathered feet so firmly planted in the grass
And a coat brushed smooth as satin, a noble head held high,
Silhouetted like a giant against the fenland sky.
What strength, allied to beauty, what dignity, what grace,
A living, breathing symbol of a sturdy, ancient race!

Oh, gentle, grave-eyed monarch, in magnificence arrayed,
May your breed continue, may your glory never fade!
For you, and all your forbears, that have ploughed our native soil,
And pulled the carts and brewers' drays, unstinting in your toil,
Are a joy and inspiration, our heritage, our pride,
Your memory for ever green throughout our countryside.
Be sure there's nothing lovelier, though ages come and go,
Than a glossy, feather-footed horse parading at the show!

THE GARDENERS

Old Miss Emma and old Miss Grace
Live in an unromantic place,
A flat in a concrete tower, so high
It almost rubs shoulders with the sky!
Tall factories loom to left and right,
With never a tree or bush in sight,
While down in the thoroughfare, grim and grey,
There's snarled-up traffic the livelong day.

Yet old Miss Emma and old Miss Grace
Live quite content in that dismal place.
They never complain of the dreary view,
For they have a garden - small, it's true,
But oh, so pretty, and oh, so bright,
It's plain to see it's their hearts' delight;
So neat, so charming, there isn't a doubt
It's watered and weeded, day in, day out!

And when the windows are opened wide
In summer, they sit there side by side,
And in fancy, the gentle pair return
To a cottage garden of flower and fern,
Where long, long ago, little Emma and Grace
Were bonnie and blithe and fair of face;
It all comes back, when the scent of stocks
Steals over the sill - from their window-box!

OLD TOM REMEMBERS

Be it early, be it late,
You'll see him at his cottage gate;
He's ninety now, if he's a day,
But loves to watch the children play.

In muffler, and an ancient cap,
He's always there, the dear old chap,
As much a part of village scene
As church tower, or the village green.

Old Tom has such a kindly eye,
A ready smile for passers-by,
And everybody, as they go,
Will wave to him, or call 'Hello!'

Around the village green, a band
Of tall and sturdy chestnuts stand,
And Tom remembers how he played
With conkers, in their autumn shade.

How long ago it seems, since he
Could run and jump, and climb a tree,
And hold his own with all his peers,
In happy, bygone, youthful years!

One day, old Tom will not be there,
Yet still, around the village square,
The little folk will laugh and play
As merry as they are today.

And round the green, where, ages gone,
Young Tom was conker champion,
The chestnut trees will raise on high
Their rose-flecked candles to the sky.

NOVEMBER

Because it's often chill and grey,
Many people, sad to say,
Do not like November ...

And yet, for some, it may possess
A certain gentle charm.
Bereft of summer's comeliness,
Bare fields, so still and calm,
And misty, against a pewter sky,
Are strangely restful to the eye.

Then, in the hedgerows linger yet
The glossiest berries, hips, and haws,
Crimson and purple, shining jet,
And bright vermilion, while the moors,
Aglow with bracken's tawny blaze,
Are lovelier than in sunny days.

And aromatic scents abound,
Mingling on the frosty air,
From little bonfires all around,
And fallen leaves, and gardens where
Tangy chrysanthemums unfold
Their petals, russet, red and gold.

And though foreshortened is the day,
When lights on every side gleam through
The early twilight's hazy blue,
In such a cosy, friendly way,
Then, in all truth, I have to say
I rather like November ...

CHRISTMAS REVERIE

Do you remember Christmas,
Long, long ago,
When the house was full of children,
Running to and fro?
When the very air was throbbing
With excitement, weeks before,
And little ones rushed, shrieking,
To the postman at the door?
When there were several stockings
To fill on Christmas night,
And a great, big, sparkling Christmas tree,
With tinsel shining bright?
When there were puddings to be stirred,
A splendid cake to ice,
And we shopped for little novelties,
Gold coins, and sugar-mice?
Do you remember Christmas,
As it was in days gone by,
With its magic and its mystery?
You do - and so do I!

Now we've a tiny Christmas tree,
To fit our tiny house,
There's not a paper-hat in sight,
Nor pretty sugar-mouse;
Just peace and quiet ... for each and all
The little ones are grown
And live in far-off places
With small children of their own.
But sometimes, when the Christmas stars
Are twinkling, how I yearn
To roll away the years, and see
Our little ones return,
Their young hearts sweet and trusting,
As they were in days gone by,
When Father Christmas drove his sleigh
Across the midnight sky .

GIFTS FOR THE CHRIST-CHILD

If called to the manger,
To visit our King,
At this present moment,
What gifts would we bring?

Not myrrh and not frankincense,
Though they smell sweet,
Nor gold - it's too wordly
To lay at His feet!

Instead, if we followed
Our hearts' inner call,
Our offerings would be
The most precious of all.

The smile on the face
Of a babe, small as He,
But rescued from famine,
Or dire poverty.

A blanket of lambs' wool,
A pillow of down,
A garland of wild flowers
To wear as a crown.

Just like the wild flowers,
Pink, yellow, and blue,
He once gave his Mother,
As little boys do.

From nations who'd promised
Their conflict to cease,
To His hands we'd carry
A white dove of peace.

And a cup, brimming over
With kindness and care,
For the lonely, the frightened,
And those in despair.

We'd fill that rough stable
With riches untold,
For love shines more brightly
Than silver or gold.

How gladly the angels
In Heaven would sing,
If such lovely tributes
We brought to our King!